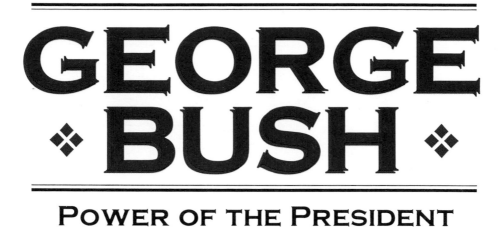

GEORGE ✦ BUSH ✦

POWER OF THE PRESIDENT

by Karen Bornemann Spies

Taking part BOOKS

ᕍP DILLON PRESS
New York

Maxwell Macmillan Canada
Toronto

Maxwell Macmillan International
New York Oxford Singapore Sydney

Photographic Acknowledgments

The photographs are reproduced through the courtesy of: The White House; University of Texas of the Permian Basin, Odessa, Texas; Susan Biddle, the White House; Carol T. Powers, the White House; Michael Sargent, the White House; David Valdez, the White House; Yale University.

Library of Congress Cataloging-in-Publication Data
Spies, Karen Bornemann.
   George Bush : Power of the President / by Karen
      Bornemann Spies.
      p.   cm. — (Taking part)
     Summary: A biography of George Herbert Walker Bush,
the forty-first president of the United States.
   ISBN 0-87518-487-1
     1. Bush, George, 1924-   —Juvenile literature.
2. Presidents-United States—Biography—Juvenile litera-
ture. [1. Bush, George, 1924-   . 2. Presidents.] I. Title.
E882.S65   1991
973.928′092—dc20   91-15862
[B]

Dillon Press
Macmillan Publishing Company
866 Third Avenue
New York, NY 10022

Maxwell Macmillan Canada, Inc.
1200 Eglinton Avenue East
Suite 200
Don Mills, Ontario M3C 3N1

Macmillan Publishing Company is part of the Maxwell Communication Group of Companies.

First edition
Printed in the United States of America
10 9 8 7 6 5 4 3 2 1

About the Author

Karen Spies is a free-lance writer and part-time ski instructor at Copper Mountain Resort in Colorado. She has written two other Taking Part biographies, *Raffi: The Children's Voice* and *Barbara Bush: Helping America Read*. The author has also written articles for many periodicals such as *Writer's Digest, Highlights, Jack and Jill, Children's Digest,* and *Child Life.*

Ms. Spies gives workshops on writing for children, as well as workshops for young writers. She lives with her husband and two children in Littleton, Colorado.

CONTENTS

INTRODUCTION

On November 8, 1988, George Herbert Walker Bush was elected the forty-first president of the United States. When he took the oath of office, he promised to serve well the people of the United States. But for George Bush, leadership began at an early age.

At Phillips Academy in Andover, Massachusetts, Bush was president of his senior class and captain of both the basketball and soccer teams. He earned his wings as a navy pilot in World War II when he was only eighteen. For his bravery in battle, Bush won the Distinguished Flying Cross. After the war, Bush married Barbara Pierce and enrolled at Yale University. By going to school during vacations as well as the regular school year, he graduated in only two and one-half years. He was an honor student and captain of Yale's championship baseball team.

Upon graduating, Bush moved to Texas and was hired by an oil company to sweep warehouses and paint machinery. He worked hard to learn everything he could about the oil business. At the age of thirty, he became president of his own firm, the Zapata Offshore Company. Zapata was so successful that it made Bush a millionaire.

After achieving success in business, George Bush entered

public life. He served four years in Congress and then was appointed to several important posts. These included ambassador to the United Nations, Republican National Committee chairman, U.S. envoy to China, and director of the Central Intelligence Agency. Bush served two terms as Ronald Reagan's vice president. Then in 1988, he became president himself.

George Bush is proud of his achievements in business and government. He is honored to serve his country. Still, personal success is not what matters most to him. His faith in God and his love of family are far more important. "The most fun I have today in my life," he has said, "is when I'm doing something with my grandchildren or with our boys and Doro [daughter Dorothy]."

A leader throughout his life—that's George Bush. A success in school, sports, military service, business, and politics, he now holds the highest office in the United States of America. He has a chance to make his own lasting mark on the country which elected him its president.

1

Shot Down!

Early on the morning of September 2, 1944, the catapult on the aircraft carrier launched the torpedo bomber into the sky. Its pilot, twenty-year-old Ensign George Bush, was part of a World War II bombing mission. An hour after takeoff, Bush spotted his target on the island of Chichi Jima and put the plane into a dive.

Suddenly there was a jolt. It felt as if a giant fist had hit the belly of the bomber. Smoke poured into the cockpit. Bush knew the plane was hit, but he stayed with his dive. He unloaded his four 500-pound bombs, helping to destroy the target. Then he pulled away and headed for the Pacific Ocean.

Once he was safely over the sea, Bush told his two

George Bush, the forty-first president of the United States, was a navy pilot during World War II.

crew members to bail out. But as Bush ejected from the plane, he hit his head and tore his parachute on the plane's tail. The rip caused the young pilot to fall fast. As he hit the water, Bush slipped out of his harness. He couldn't see his two crewmen or his safety raft.

Just then an airplane swooped down toward the waves and dipped its wings. It was Bush's squadron leader, Don Melvin, signaling the raft's location. Bush swam to the raft and scrambled inside. He had no food or water, and his head was bleeding where the bomber's tail had gashed it. He couldn't find any oars for the raft, so he paddled with his hands.

Japanese boats had left the island and moved out to capture him. But a squadron buddy, Doug West, and several other fighter pilots showered the Japanese boats with bullets and drove them away. West had seen Bush's bleeding head, so he flew back over the raft and dropped a medical kit. Then he had to return to the carrier, leaving Bush alone on the sea.

The young ensign worried about what had happened to his crewmen. Later Bush learned that one of them had gone down with the plane. The other had jumped but his parachute had failed to open.

The wind and waves pushed the raft back toward the island, which was occupied by the Japanese. Bush spent a few hours wondering if he would be rescued.

Suddenly a submarine surfaced near his raft. Bush felt a stab of panic—what if it was Japanese? Crewmen came out on the forward deck. "Welcome aboard," one of them called. The sailor was an American—the sub was the USS *Finback*. Bush was safe!

For completing this mission, George Bush earned the Distinguished Flying Cross. He served in the navy until the war ended in 1945. Forty-three years later, he began serving his country in another way, as the forty-first president of the United States.

George Herbert Walker Bush was born in Milton, Massachusetts, on June 12, 1924. He was the second of five children born to Prescott Bush, Sr., and Dorothy Walker Bush. George was named after his mother's father, George Herbert Walker. Grandfather Walker was nicknamed Pop, so George was soon called Little Pop or Poppy.

On his mother's side, George's family was wealthy and powerful. Grandfather Walker owned a financial investment firm and founded the Walker Cup, a prize for the world's best amateur golfer. On his plantation in South Carolina, the family hunted and rode horses.

The Bush side of the family was equally well-to-do. Samuel P. Bush, George's grandfather, was president of a steel company. George's father, Prescott Bush,

Sr., was a Wall Street investment banker and served in the U.S. Senate between 1952 and 1963.

George grew up in Greenwich, Connecticut, one of the wealthiest cities in the United States. He lived in an eight-bedroom house with his older brother, Prescott (Pres); younger brothers Jonathan and William (Bucky); and sister, Nancy. Three maids, a cook, and a handyman and chauffeur helped Mrs. Bush run the household.

Although George's parents came from wealthy families, they refused to spoil their children. George says that he learned about duty and service from his father. Strict but loving, Mr. Bush believed in hard work. He felt that the more advantages a person had, the more he or she should help others.

Dorothy Walker Bush raised the children to be thoughtful and kind. George credits her with teaching him how to get along with others. From his mother,

Eighteen-month-old George picks flowers in the garden.

George also got his sense of humor and his modesty. She didn't let the Bush children brag about themselves.

The idea of sharing and helping others left its mark on George at an early age. He always offered to share half of what he had—food, toys, clothes—with friends and family members. This earned him another nickname, Have Half.

The family enjoyed many summers together at Walker's Point in Kennebunkport, Maine. George grew to love the sea and the rocky Maine coast. He says his Maine summers were "the best of all possible adventures." Part of the adventure was learning to fish. Grandfather Walker taught all his grandchildren to use a basic green line with a small piece of cloth tied to it.

Grandfather Walker also taught George and Pres how to handle and dock his lobster boat, *Tomboy*. When George was nine and Pres was eleven, their grandfather let them take *Tomboy* out into the ocean by themselves. A sudden storm blew up. The strong winds and the white-capped waves scared the boys. When George and Pres brought the boat in safely, Grandfather Walker was proud of them. George says, "That gave me confidence that's lasted all my life."

The Bushes were an athletic, competitive family. Grandfather Walker had been amateur heavyweight champ of Missouri and in the 1920s was president of the United States Golf Association. George's father had been amateur golf champion of Ohio and captain of the Yale University baseball team. His mother was an excellent tennis player and golfer. Full of energy, she enjoyed playing baseball and basketball with her children and often beat them in foot races.

Even though they were competitive, George's parents were caring. George says that as he was growing up, they were always there when he needed them. "It taught me to be the same way with my own children," he recalls.

Religious teaching was also important at the Bush home. George's father or mother read aloud from the Bible at breakfast. The family attended services at Christ Church, an Episcopal church in Greenwich.

The Bush boys all went to Greenwich Country Day School, a private school near their home. George was a good student but not an outstanding one. He excelled at sports, playing both soccer and baseball. In winter, he enjoyed ice hockey as well as sledding on the hillside behind the school building. Sometimes the teachers watered down the sled run to make it fast and icy. George and his friends tried to see who could make the most runs before the recess bell rang.

When George graduated from day school, his father sent him to Phillips Academy, in Andover, Massachusetts. Known as Andover, it is a very fine college preparatory school. George's grades were average, but he earned honors in other areas. He was captain of the soccer and basketball teams and also played baseball. In his senior year, George was elected class president and secretary of the student council. He held more leadership positions than anyone else in his graduating class of two hundred students.

After graduation in 1942, George joined the navy. The United States had entered World War II after the Japanese attacked Pearl Harbor on December 7, 1941, and George wanted to serve his country. But he also wanted freedom from the pressure of being his father's son. Prescott, Sr., was a leader and admired by everyone, and George wanted to begin his own life apart from his successful father.

After finishing training in North Carolina and Texas, George became a junior officer in June 1943. At eighteen, he was the youngest pilot in the navy.

U.S. Navy pilot George Bush.

When George went to war, he left behind a girl he cared about very much. At a Christmas dance in 1941, he had met sixteen-year-old Barbara Pierce. Her father was Marvin Pierce, chairman of the McCall Corporation, which published *Redbook* and *McCall's* magazines.

George painted Barbara's name on his plane, a TBM Avenger torpedo bomber. For a year and a half, he flew combat missions against the Japanese in the South Pacific. After his 1944 crash landing, he spent a month on the submarine that had rescued him. The sub had to complete its missions before returning George to his carrier, the *San Jacinto*. While aboard the sub, George thought about what he wanted to do with his life. He didn't understand why he had survived the crash while his crew members had not. But he was thankful for a second chance to make something of his life.

George and Barbara before they were married, with George's youngest brother, Bucky.

In December 1944, George and the rest of the crew of the "San Jack" were sent home. George returned to Greenwich on Christmas Eve. He was thankful to be home with his family and his sweetheart. On January 6, 1945, George and Barbara were married in "Bar's" family church in Rye, New York.

George was reassigned to a base in Norfolk, Virginia, where he trained new torpedo-bomber pilots. He and Barbara lived in a house in nearby Virginia Beach, which they shared with three other couples.

On August 14, 1945, the Japanese agreed to surrender, ending World War II. The streets of Virginia Beach filled with families celebrating the victory. George and Barbara joined in, but later went to a nearby church to give thanks for the war's end.

George Bush was discharged from the navy in September 1945. Two months later he entered Yale University, part of a long family tradition. Other Yale graduates in his family included his great-grandfather; his father; his older brother, Pres; and four uncles.

At Yale University, George studied economics and was a standout in sports. He played soccer for one season and baseball for three. In his senior year, he was named captain of the baseball team, which

Barbara and George's wedding day.

George Bush (on the right), *captain of the varsity baseball team, welcomes the legendary Babe Ruth at a pre-game ceremony in 1948 at the Yale University Field.*

twice played in the finals of the college World Series.

On July 6, 1946, George Walker Bush, the first of George and Barbara's six children, was born. The three of them lived in an old house that had been divided into thirteen tiny apartments for war veterans and their wives.

Like many veterans, George Bush was in a hurry to finish school. Though young in years, George felt mature in outlook, and he had a family to support. Although it usually takes four years to complete a college degree, George earned his in less than three years. Because of his excellent grades, he was elected to Phi Beta Kappa, an honor society. When he graduated in 1948, George was 24.

Because of George's family background and education, his father's firm offered him a position. But George and Barbara agreed that he should not join his father's business. Even though he loved and admired his father, George said, "We wanted to make our own way, our own mistakes, and shape our own future." George and Barbara decided to seek their fortune in the West. The place they chose was Texas.

2

Life in the Oil Fields

In June 1948 George Bush headed for Odessa, Texas, driving his red two-door Studebaker. He stopped to eat and ordered his first West Texas-style lunch: chicken-fried steak. George wondered if it would be a steak fried like a chicken, or a chicken fried like a steak? It turned out to be a steak covered in a creamy chicken gravy. Chicken-fried steak became one of George's favorite foods.

Although George liked West Texas food, he wasn't sure if he belonged in Texas. It was hot and windy, with few trees. But he knew that underneath the dry soil was a fortune in oil. George wanted to learn about the oil business, make money, and shape his own future.

Odessa, Texas, in 1950.

During his navy career, George had saved three thousand dollars. He and Barbara figured this was enough for them to get started on their own, without borrowing from their families. They moved into a shabby shotgun house, so called because it was long and narrow like the box which contains a shotgun. A thin partition divided the house into two small apartments. George and Barbara's apartment had one bedroom, a tiny kitchen, and a bathroom that they shared with their neighbors.

George got his first oil company job from a close family friend, Neil Mallon, who was president of Dresser Industries. George began as an equipment clerk, sweeping out warehouses and painting oil-drilling machinery. Often the machines had been sitting in the sun for weeks, and painting them, said George, was like riding a hot branding iron without a saddle.

In 1949 George was promoted to a better position and became a drilling-tools salesman in California. For a year, he traveled about one thousand miles each week, selling parts for oil drills. While in California, the Bush family lived in five different cities.

George and Barbara's second child was born in Compton, California, in December 1949. They named her Pauline Robinson Bush, after Barbara's mother. Her nickname was Robin, since she was as lively as one of those little birds.

Shortly after Robin's birth, Dresser Industries transferred George back to Texas. The Bushes settled in Midland, in a small house on "Easter Egg Row." All the houses on the street were the same, so the builder painted each one a bright color. The Bush family's "Easter egg" was light blue.

The Bushes made many friends during the Midland years. Most had come from different parts of the country, hoping to make their fortunes in oil. Each Sunday after church, many of them got together for a hamburger cookout and games.

Both George and Barbara were active in their community. Barbara helped groups that were working to build better hospitals, schools, and museums. George taught Sunday school at theFirst Presbyterian Church and served as a director of the Midland Bank. He was a popular Little League baseball coach, who amazed the kids with his knowledge of the sport and his athletic skills. One player recalled that George could put his glove behind his back, drop his head forward, and catch the ball behind his back.

Midland was in the heart of the new oil boom, and George was caught up in the excitement. He decided to go into business on his own as a wildcatter—a person who buys rights to drill for oil on private property, hoping to find oil in a territory not known to contain any. Sometimes wildcatters found oil and got rich, but other times they lost everything. The stakes were high, but so was the reward. George was sure these risks would pay off.

But he worried about how to break the news to his boss and good friend, Neil Mallon. Mallon listened to George's plans and then said quietly, "I really hate to see you go, George, but if I were your age, I'd be doing the same thing—and here's how I'd go about it."

For half an hour, Neil Mallon talked as George wrote on a yellow pad of paper. He gave George many excellent ideas about how to organize and run an independent oil company. George says Mallon taught him a lesson he's never forgotten, "that whenever anyone working for you wants to move on, don't stand in the way. Lend a hand."

In 1951 George and his neighbor, John Overbey,

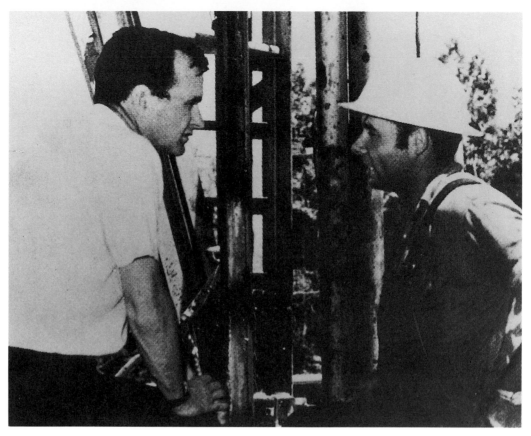

George Bush in the oil fields in Texas.

founded the Bush-Overbey Oil Development Company, Inc., which sold oil and gas properties. George's uncle, Herbie Walker, loaned them start-up money.

The Bush-Overbey offices were next to those of Bill and Hugh Liedkte, fellow oil operators. In 1953 Bush-Overbey joined with the Liedktes to form Zapata

Petroleum Corporation. Zapata located and bought oil-producing land. George was only twenty-nine years old when he helped to found Zapata.

Just as the new company began to prosper, tragedy struck the Bush family. Lively three-year-old Robin became very tired. She didn't want to play, and her appetite was poor. Barbara Bush took Robin to their family doctor, Dorothy Wyvell, who ran many tests. The tests showed that Robin had leukemia, a deadly blood disease. The disease had spread throughout her body, and she had very little time left to live. The doctor felt the best thing to do was take Robin home and make her as comfortable as possible.

The Bushes felt they had to try to help Robin. In those days, little was known about leukemia. They took her to Memorial Hospital in New York City for special treatment. Barbara stayed there with Robin while George flew back and forth between New York and Texas. George tried to be both father and mother to George W., who was seven, and to Jeb, who was only a few months old. But whenever he flew to New York, he had to leave the children with neighbors. Prayer became an increasingly important part of the Bushes' lives at this time.

During the six months that she was in the hospital, Robin sometimes seemed to get better. But the disease was too powerful. She died just before her fourth birthday.

George has often said that he and Barbara helped each other face this terrible loss. Robin's death brought them closer together. Their faith in God helped both of them feel stronger. As George stated, "You learn what faith is." In facing the sadness of Robin's death, George was even more sure of his desire to serve others.

The Bushes missed Robin terribly, and nothing

could replace her. But they were cheered by George W. and baby John Ellis, known as Jeb because of his initials. In the next few years, the Bushes were blessed with three more children: Neil, Marvin, and Dorothy ("Doro").

As the family grew, so did George's business success. In 1954 he and his partners separated their onshore (land) drilling operations from their off-shore (sea) operations. They formed Zapata Offshore Company to handle the riskier offshore operations. George, only thirty years old, was named president of the new company. He moved his family and the company headquarters to Houston, Texas, which had become the financial center for the oil industry.

George and Barbara had gone to Texas to start a new life. They had made many friends and built a strong family life. Now they were ready to face new challenges together.

3

Victories and Defeats

George Bush had proven his business skills. He had saved enough money to take care of his children's educations. Yet he began to feel that success in business wasn't enough. He wanted to become a more important member of the community, as his father had done. Prescott Bush, Sr., served as a U.S. senator for ten years. By the time the elder Bush retired in 1963, George had begun thinking about a career in politics, too.

Although George continued to work in the oil business, in 1962 he became chairman of the Republican party in Harris County, Texas. Over the years, the Republican party had looked out for the interests of business, and George, as a successful

George and Barbara in Houston, Texas, on victory night of the congressional campaign in 1966.

businessman, fit right in. The Republican party was growing in Texas, but the majority of Texans still belonged to the Democratic party.

In 1964 George ran for the U.S. Senate against Democrat Ralph Yarborough, who held the office. George campaigned hard but lost. Even so, he won 43.5 percent of the vote. No other Republican candidate had ever done that well in Texas.

It was tough to lose. But George Bush handled his loss the way he'd handled his other problems: He got busy. Barbara Bush recalls, "He was wonderful. He got right on the phone the next morning and thanked everybody who helped him . . . cheering them up."

Bush's co-workers couldn't understand his interest in politics. Why run for office when he already had an interesting, high-paying job? George has written, "In Midland I was bitten by the bug that led me into the oil business. Now I'd been bitten by another bug."

The Bush family in 1964. The children seated on the sofa are Dorothy and Marvin. George Walker is seated on the arm of the sofa. The children standing are Neil (on the left) and Jeb.

Public service, he believed, was a way to make a better state and a better country.

George thought hard about the next step to take in his political career. Instead of trying to do both business and politics, he sold his interest in Zapata in

February 1966. The sale made him a millionaire. George then devoted his time to running for Congress. He easily won the election that November and became the representative from the Seventh Congressional District of Houston, Texas.

The Bushes moved to Washington, D.C. George and Barbara were determined to stay close as a family. They continued to invite friends to backyard barbecues, and on weekends George scheduled special time with each of his five children. No matter how busy their dad was, he always talked to them when they called his office.

George was the first freshman (first-term) congressperson in sixty years to be named to the House Ways and Means Committee. It is often called the most powerful committee in the House of Representatives, because all tax laws originate there.

The late 1960s were challenging years to be a

member of Congress. The United States was at war in Southeast Asia, trying to keep communist North Vietnam from taking over weaker South Vietnam. George felt the United States should help any government fighting against the Communists, but not everyone agreed.

Another important issue dividing America was civil rights. Although he was not a major leader in the fight against racial discrimination, George voted in favor of the Fair Housing Act of 1968. It allowed people of any race to live where they wanted. Most voters in George's district were against open housing.

After the vote, George received hate letters and death threats. He defended his beliefs before a booing audience in Houston. He stated firmly, ". . . a man should not have a door slammed in his face because he is a Negro or speaks with a Latin American accent. Open housing offers a ray of hope for blacks and other minorities." His listeners sensed the strength of George's beliefs and gave him an ovation.

In 1970 George took on another challenge. He resigned his congressional seat to run for the Senate against democrat Lloyd Bentsen. George campaigned hard and won more than a million votes. But he still lost the election.

After the loss, President Nixon appointed him ambassador to the United Nations (UN) in New York City. The UN is an international organization of countries working together to solve world problems such as hunger, disease, and war. Some people doubted that George knew enough about foreign affairs, but he listened, learned, and made friends with many delegates. He soon earned praise for his peacemaking work among arguing nations.

While George was at the UN, his father became ill with lung cancer. When Prescott Bush died on

October 8, 1972, George said he had lost his best friend.

In January 1973, President Nixon asked George to take charge of the Republican National Committee. He was considered a "loyal party man," and Nixon counted on his support. But then Nixon became implicated in the Watergate scandal, named after the Watergate building near the White House. In the spring of 1972, seven men had broken into the Watergate offices of the Democratic National Committee. They stole important papers and planted electronic listening devices there.

As the scandal grew, it became clear that the president and several of his top staff members were involved. On August 7, 1974, George Bush wrote to President Nixon. He strongly urged the president to resign, since this would be best for the country. Two days later, Nixon resigned and Vice President Gerald

Ford succeeded him as president. George Bush was mentioned as a possibility for vice president. He wanted the job, but instead Ford chose Nelson Rockefeller, the former governor of New York.

After the Watergate scandal and being passed over for the vice presidency, George was disappointed. He and Barbara felt as if they needed to spend some time away from Washington. When President Ford offered him the choice of working in England, France, or China, George chose China. President Ford named him the chief envoy, or United States representative, in Beijing, the capital of the People's Republic of China. George and Barbara were excited about the challenge of working in the Far East.

The Bushes arrived in Beijing in October 1974. They enjoyed getting to know the Chinese people and their leaders. Barbara studied Chinese art and history. They both stopped using their official car and delighted the Chinese by riding bicycles like ordinary citizens. The Chinese called them "the Bushers, who ride bicycles just as Chinese do."

Before long, the Bushes were packing their suitcases again. President Ford wanted George to take over as director of the Central Intelligence Agency (CIA), the government agency that handles all secret information related to national security. It was a difficult decision. George was concerned that if he took the CIA job, the Chinese would think he had spied on them all along. But George felt he couldn't say no to the president.

George arrived back in Washington, D.C., in 1976, to find the CIA in trouble for illegally spying on United States citizens. George fired some agency administrators and promoted others. He worked with the president to form a list of rules to keep future CIA operations more honest.

But the job was frustrating. He couldn't talk about his top secret work with Barbara. They couldn't go to Washington social events, because the CIA director could have nothing to do with politics. George decided he wanted to return to politics, so he resigned from the CIA in 1977.

Suddenly George was jobless for the first time since leaving college. He served on several committees, but he actually spent most of the next two years running for president.

Barbara and George in China in 1974.

The Bush family in 1979. Top row, from left to right: Marvin; George (age 3); Jeb; George Bush; George Walker; George Walker's wife, Laura. Bottom row, left to right: Jeb's wife, Columba; Noelle (age 2); Dorothy; Barbara Bush; Neil.

4

A Heartbeat Away

In 1977 George and Barbara returned to Houston and began to think about their future. George had been in government service for fifteen years, taking many leadership roles. He had strong family values and knew his own abilities. He felt America needed a president who believed in the people—someone like him.

By the middle of 1978 George had formed a campaign staff headed by his good friend Jim Baker. George and his staff began to give speeches and raise money all across the United States. Barbara Bush and their five children helped. On May 1, 1979, George Bush formally announced that he was running for the 1980 Republican presidential nomination.

George ran a grassroots campaign, meaning that he liked to get out and meet people. He believes "that nothing beats personal, eye-to-eye contact in a political campaign—not just talking to people, but listening to what they have to say." Because of his combined government and business experience, he said he was the best candidate. Bush's campaign slogan was "A President You Won't Have to Train."

The Bush election team worked hard. But George lost the nomination to Ronald Reagan, whose experience as a movie actor made him a warm, natural speaker. In July 1980, Ronald Reagan chose George Bush to be his vice-presidential running mate. Both Reagan and Bush campaigned hard and were elected four months later.

On January 20, 1981, George Bush was inaugurated as the vice president of the United States. In the past, the vice president had been somewhat of an outsider in the White House. But President Reagan changed that. He went out of his way to include George in important White House meetings. Their fierce campaign rivalry had changed into a friendly, trusting partnership.

Still, Bush could not shake his public image as a "wimp." His nasal speaking voice and unwavering support of President Reagan made Bush look weak. Some reporters said he didn't have enough spunk to give his own opinions. But Bush believed that an important part of the vice presidential role was to support the president. When he disagreed with President Reagan, he told him privately.

Their weekly private lunches offered George the perfect opportunity to share his views with the president, especially on relations with other countries. Since the presidency was Reagan's first national position, George Bush had more experience in foreign affairs. They met each Thursday at the White House, eating outdoors if the weather was nice. Since both men love Mexican food, lunch often consisted of tortilla chips and salsa and cheese soup or chili.

It is often said that the vice president is "only a heartbeat away from the presidency." He or she must be ready to become president at a moment's notice if the president dies, resigns, or is removed from office. During the eight years that George Bush was vice president, two emergencies brought him a heartbeat away from becoming president of the United States.

On March 31, 1981, only seventy days into Reagan's first term, the president was shot as he was leaving the Hilton Hotel. The gunman had fired six shots at the president and those with him, wounding three of the people. Vice President Bush was flying to Texas to make a speech when he received a message telling him to return to Washington immediately.

Bush and his advisers agreed that he should meet in an emergency session with the cabinet and the National Security Council. It was necessary to show the world that the government of the United States was in full operation, even though the president was hospitalized.

For the next two days, George took President Reagan's place. He ran a cabinet meeting and met with congressional leaders. But he continued to use his own office and would not sit in the president's chair. "The president is still president," he told the cabinet. He was praised for the way he filled in for President Reagan.

Four years later, on July 13, 1985, there was another national emergency. Bush was named acting president of the United States while Reagan had cancer surgery. He was the first person ever to be named acting president. The power of the presidency was returned to Reagan as soon as he awoke from surgery.

As vice president, Bush traveled to more than seventy foreign countries and served as president of the U.S. Senate. As head of a task force to end unnecessary government regulations, George Bush won public notice. His task force on reducing crime and drug smuggling in southern Florida was less successful, since drug imports continued to increase. A third task force made a popular suggestion: The United States should not make any agreements with terrorists.

Yet, this recommendation was ignored during the Iran-contra affair. Military weapons were secretly sold to Iran. Some American officials hoped the sales would gain the release of seven hostages held by the Iranian government. The money from the arms sales was given to the rebel forces, or "contras," in Nicaragua.

This was done secretly, since Congress had voted to decrease the amount of money the U.S. government sent to the contras. Thus, the whole affair was illegal. It brought shame to the United States. Why did the government deal with Iran when Iranians held American hostages? Why were the wishes of Congress ignored?

Some newspaper writers and political leaders felt Vice President Bush must have known about the Iran-contra affair. But he has stated many times that he was not involved. He was also too loyal to President Reagan to say in public that he would have acted differently.

Political opponents of George Bush thought that the Iran-contra affair would harm his chances to be elected president. But they soon learned that they were wrong.

5

The Road Ahead

Before a United States presidential election, a Democratic and a Republican candidate are each chosen through a series of state elections known as primaries. George Bush won all the important Republican primary elections, so he was nominated as the 1988 Republican candidate for the presidency. He chose as his running mate Senator J. Danforth ("Dan") Quayle. The young-looking Quayle was only forty-one years old and was not well known outside of his home state, Indiana.

Many people did not like Bush's choice. After twelve years in Congress, Quayle was just beginning to make his mark. During the Vietnam War, he had used the power of his wealthy family and joined the

George Bush and his running mate, Dan Quayle.

National Guard to avoid being drafted for combat duty. Service in the guard was legal. But it did not look good to voters, especially since Quayle had been a strong supporter of the military when in Congress. The Bush-Quayle ticket seemed to be in trouble.

But Bush refused to drop Quayle. He followed his own advice in sticking to his choice: "Do your best and don't look back."

He declared, "I mean to win. I seek the presidency to build a better America." During the campaign, Bush promised not to raise taxes. He pledged to create new jobs, to spend more for new school programs, and to crack down on drug pushers. He told voters he would continue the peace and prosperity of the Reagan years.

The Democratic party nominated Massachusetts governor Michael Dukakis as its presidential candidate. He chose Senator Lloyd Bentsen of Texas as his vice-presidential running mate. Bentsen was the person who had defeated George Bush in his first Senate race in Texas.

From the beginning of the campaign, Bush attacked Dukakis. He said that Dukakis was wrong to veto a Massachusetts law that required children to say the Pledge of Allegiance each day in the schools. Bush used the flag episodes to try to make Dukakis look unpatriotic. Instead of explaining himself, Dukakis attacked Bush by saying ". . . in my judgment he's not fit to hold office."

Many Americans criticized both Bush and Dukakis for ignoring campaign issues. The two candidates seemed more interested in verbally attacking each other than they did in proposing solutions to problems such as arms control, drugs, and homelessness. Voter turnout on election day, November 8, 1988, was the lowest in a presidential election since 1924.

George came out the winner and was sworn into office on January 20, 1989. Two hundred years ago, the first president of the United States was inaugurated. When George Bush took the oath of office, he put his left hand on the Bible used at George Washington's inauguration, as well as on the Bush family Bible.

The Bushes love their busy life. Each day they awaken to country music as early as 5:00 A.M. They drink coffee and juice in bed while they watch and discuss the news. A staff member has said that talking with Mrs. Bush helps clear the president's mind.

Even though they now live in the White House, the Bushes have kept their down-to-earth manner. Neither one buys expensive designer clothing. Their dog, Millie, sleeps with them, and they wash her in their shower.

Americans have grown to admire the Bushes' strong marriage and George's close relationship with

Inauguration Day, January 20, 1989.

his wife. The president has confessed, "I couldn't live without her, and she couldn't live without me."

Barbara Bush has helped her husband look closer at social and health problems in the United States. When George was vice president, Barbara visited patients with AIDS. She convinced him to add more government money for fighting the disease. Her interest in children and reading influenced George's promise to be the "education president." Bush feels that Barbara has "set a good example in a lot of volunteer action."

The Bushes have kept their strong family ties. The president has often said that his greatest success in life is that his five children "still come home." Now he also enjoys having his grandchildren running and playing in the halls of the White House.

Family vacations are often spent at Kennebunkport. The president enjoys speeding over the waves in

The Bush family today.

his twenty-eight-foot powerboat, *Fidelity*. Left-handed Bush likes to play golf, but uses right-handed clubs. Friends joke that his golf games are aerobic exercise because he walks around the course so rapidly. On Sundays President and Mrs. Bush go to St. Ann's Episcopal Church with their family. Sometimes they combine business and pleasure by entertaining foreign visitors at the Maine vacation home.

Although he works very hard, President Bush enjoys his free time. When he moved into the White House, he had a horseshoes pit dug. Horseshoes is a game for two or four players. The aim is to toss a U-shaped iron horseshoe around a short metal stake located forty feet away. Bush plays on a horseshoes team with his son Marvin.

His favorite television show is "NFL Monday Night Football," and his favorite magazine is a fishing journal called *Bassmaster*. Bush cheers for the Houston Astros baseball team, which he began watching in the 1960s when he lived in Texas. The president keeps fit by jogging. Like Presidents Ford and Carter, he often uses the White House tennis courts. Although he is left-handed, he plays tennis right-handed, the way his mother taught him.

The president's favorite foods include Chinese food from take-out restaurants and Tex-Mex dishes

President Bush jogs to keep fit.

such as chili. He dislikes many green vegetables, especially broccoli. When he became president, George Bush refused to have broccoli served at any of his meals. California farmers quickly sent him ten tons of broccoli. The Bushes laughed about it and donated the food to Washington, D.C., food banks.

This, then, is our forty-first president: six feet, two inches tall, well educated, and experienced in politics and business. He is honest and trustworthy, with an excellent record in government.

But some people felt that he never stayed at one post long, until he was elected vice president. In this position, he carried out the orders of someone else. As president, would he be able to lead?

Both at home and abroad, George Bush has shown leadership. He acted quickly to fill a vacancy on the U.S. Supreme Court. Bush supported legislation to provide money, jobs, and other help for those who are handicapped. Meetings between President Bush and Soviet leader Mikhail Gorbachev have begun a new era of cooperation between the United States and the Soviet Union. President Bush and Canada's Prime Minister Brian Mulroney formed a committee to find ways to cut down on pollution.

President Bush and Soviet leader Mikhail Gorbachev in a meeting to promote cooperation between the United States and the Soviet Union.

Their agreement builds on new air-quality goals already written into U.S. law by the Clean Air Act that Bush signed on November 15, 1990.

Still, Bush has not met all of his campaign promises. Public schools need more money and better teachers. Bush raised taxes in 1990 because it was hard to cut government spending enough to meet the budget. The economy and number of new jobs haven't grown as rapidly as he hoped they would.

Problems have developed with many savings and loan companies, known as S & Ls. They had lent money to businesses that could not repay what they owed. Eventually the S & Ls ran out of money and the taxpayers had to repay this debt. The president's son Neil was an adviser to an S & L. He said he did not know of any illegal activities. But many people were unhappy with President Bush because of his son's actions.

In the summer of 1990, Bush faced a problem in the Middle East. On August 2, Iraq invaded Kuwait, which supplies oil to the United States. Bush sent troops to nearby Saudi Arabia to protect its oil fields. President Bush said he did not want war, but Iraq's President Saddam Hussein refused to withdraw his army from Kuwait. The United Nations passed a resolution authorizing force against Hussein.

When Hussein refused to withdraw, Bush ordered the American-led allied forces to bomb Iraq beginning on January 17, 1991. The force, the largest since World War II, completely destroyed the Iraqi army's fighting ability. Because of President Bush's firm actions in the Persian Gulf War, public opinion of him reached its highest level.

The challenge for George Bush will be to retain his popularity after interest in the war dies down. Will he turn the same energy he directed on the war toward solving problems at home? Can he improve the nations' schools, lessen crime in the cities, and reduce drug use?

President Bush has shown that he can make tough decisions. He has faith in America's ability to solve its problems, and he wants to continue to take a leading role in this process. In the words of his 1989 inaugural speech, "A new breeze is blowing—and a nation refreshed by freedom stands ready to move on. . . . I do not fear what is ahead. For our problems are large, but our heart is larger. Our challenges are great, but our will is greater. . . ."

Important Dates

1924	Born on June 12 in Milton, Massachusetts, the second son of Prescott Bush, Sr., and Dorothy Walker Bush.
1942	Graduated from Phillips Academy in Andover, Massachusetts. Enlisted in United States Navy.
1942-1945	Served as a navy pilot during World War II.
1945	On January 6, married Barbara Pierce in Rye, New York.
1946	Birth of eldest son, George Walker Bush.
1948	Graduated from Yale University with a degree in economics. Moved to Odessa, Texas.
1948-1950	Oilfield-supply salesman for Dresser Industries/ IDECO.
1949	Birth of first daughter, Pauline Robinson (Robin) Bush.
1951-1953	Co-founder of Bush-Overbey Oil Development Company.
1953	Birth of second son, John Ellis (Jeb) Bush.
1953	Co-founder of Zapata Petroleum Corporation.
1953	Death of three-year-old Robin Bush.
1954-1966	President of Zapata Offshore Company.
1955	Birth of third son, Neil Mallon Bush.
1956	Birth of fourth son, Marvin Pierce Bush.
1959	Birth of second daughter, Dorothy Walker (Doro) Bush.
1964	Lost U.S. Senate race to Democrat Ralph Yarborough.

1967-1971	Served in the House of Representatives from the Seventh Congressional District of Houston, Texas.
1970	Lost race for U.S. Senate to Democrat Lloyd Bentsen.
1971-1973	Served as United States ambassador to the United Nations.
1973-1974	Served as chairman of the Republican National Committee.
1974-1975	Served as chief of the United States Liaison Office in the People's Republic of China.
1976-1977	Served as director of the Central Intelligence Agency.
1977-1979	Campaigned for the Republican nomination to the United States presidency.
1980	Became Ronald Reagan's vice-presidential running mate.
1981-1988	Served as vice president of the United States.
1987	Began second campaign for the presidency on October 12.
1988	On November 8, elected president of the United States.
1989	Inaugurated as the forty-first president of the United States on January 20.
1991	On January 17, ordered U.S.-led allied forces to begin attack on Iraq.
1991	Declared victory over Iraq on February 27.

INDEX